DOGGERLAND

DOGGERLAND

ANCESTRAL POEMS

by Dicko King

Off the Grid Press
Somerville, Massachusetts

ACKNOWLEDGEMENTS

This book is for Treva, my first listener.

I am grateful for the time and caring attention given me by Miguel Murphy, Jeannine Savard, Norman Dubie, and Cynthia Hogue.

With love for Mary Alice McCarthy King and Richard King, their forebears and descendants. And for my cousins, for my brothers—for my children and for theirs . . .

This would not be the book it is without the careful attention of the editors, Tam Lin Neville and Bert Stern. I am indebted to them both.

"Smuggler" was previously published in *Portland Review*.

I am indebted to my great-grandfather, James Berry for some of his stories which were compiled and edited by Gertude M. Horgan as *Tales of the West of Ireland* for The Dolmen Press (December 1966), Dublin, Ireland. I have relied on these tales for inspiration and family history. There are notes on page 93 of this book on quotes used from Berry.

Off the Grid Press
24 Quincy Street
Somerville, MA 02143
http://offthegridpress.net

Interior design by Michael Alpert. Cover design by Dicko King and Michael Alpert. Printed by Cushing-Malloy, Inc., Ann Arbor, Michigan.

ISBN 978-0-9778429-7-1

For our father, Richard King 1916–2007

Contents

TOWNLANDS

DEATH AT DOO LOUGH

KATHLEEN

NOTES   93

DOGGERLAND

During and after the last Ice Age, until about 6500 BCE, the North Sea lowered, and exposed a landmass which connected Great Britain to mainland Europe. Doggerland was a verdant tundra hunted and fished by ancient peoples. In 2009, a skull fragment of a Neandertal was dredged up from that underwater homeland.

Winter Grass

This Thursday,
death cut the weedy grass in half.

Death again this morning in the yard, loudly
crushing leaves.

I wish his scythe was not an old grandchild's memory—

    forget, forgot . . . forgotten.

Gromastoon

*. . . The Gromastoons took their name
from an unpalatable wild potato.*

I sit on Turlin Strand, down from John Berry's ruins.
Blood of the old sea kings of the Owles in my veins,
blood of the relentless Gromastoons, and
of their relentless foe, the Galvanaghs

—South Boston cabbie's blood—
the Hennessey cop's, and that of Kathleen,
my father's mother—our lifeblood.

And we named our children
without a thought for histories . . .

and word of mouth dies
with the old packman, Malley, Patrick of Shraugh
buried by his grandson, James Berry, father to Kathleen,
in Murrisk Abbey at the foot of the limestone altar;
beneath him, his grandfather, the smuggler,
Shemus Fodda alongside

the wild woman, Una O'Fergus,
mother of three Augustinians.

It is a long time since all the telling stopped
   '. . . and Fergus girls drove poets into exile.'

MUD

Cambrian Sea

The old Mud,
less sea than soup,
came before we
and they.

Might we have been
sisters when, in rows
of boxy starts we
learned dry law,
made imprints
wet as fish
—*before fish?*

Kept lessons learned
for hearts or minds
in jellied eggs
and therm.

We gained
advantage
then, as with us in:
   Us not them.

Our fortune at the dug
of mud-borne luck,
and at the expense
of each beast
or slug unlucky
to have met us.

Fesh

Connacht men, even our new boys,
would have the first fish out of water
one of us.

But it was another.

She was footed from the start,
and gorgeous legs they were,
slick as mud, and her armored
head blistered with teeth.

She was game for a walk.

No beauty, no hagfish either,
and elbows—a hint of them, and
oily finger nubs knuckling in
and under till she was up—
a lovely smile back to
her swiveled
neck

—a fish with a neck.

Not jawless or boney-headed,
but flex. *Oh . . . there was sex there*

in that beguiling twist she took,
that belly flop she made
in Africa.

Greenbottle

Those bog men, waxen, eggs in their eyes,
were planted in the ground to grow
in sacrifice, or simply blamed,
cut like sheep, they seep still
into the memory collective,
unsettling as flies.

It's hidden in the head
—this missed communion with the other
—in that wet root mistook for stone.

It's hidden in their sacrifice
—the sacramental sheared and strewn
as if, asunder, they are not a part of us

—those bones of theirs de-sanctified.

There are those of us still gray on this
—are loathe to have opinion.

Look at the untidy business
of indifference in the world today

—or look at the maggot and his worry
bother mither,

the greenbottle fly, aroost
in the wounds of sheep.

—Now, imagine yourself free from blame.

Little Tawny Rabbit Boy

Not yet sloth-or-monkey-like
—no legs yet, or arms to have akimbo;
rather more skim than lather, a thin
membrane adrowned in the kit
of a womb new to his purposes
—which were complex. Imagine
his dreaming as he hung
with his imagination
onto the limbo
of a now forgotten forest
of first woman—him

waiting to become airborne—just born
out of the first whomever—who might mourn
him if he strangled, might not have
as she squatted, emptied the womb—
she, first ever on the ground, wet
leaves sticking to the bottoms
of her hard, bald feet,
branches snapping above, below,
in small goodbyes.

—And the birthing, easy
as the two dimensions
—without our 3rd—
that concept new, the pain
not written yet, nor is any law
or Wound or Penalty of being.

Or that *to be* just *was*
and only later grew contrarily
alongside its opposing forces.

The lot of them went upright, straightened
—out of gazing skyward, reaching
up. Her milk dried. They bred
and died, bred and died until

the little tawny rabbit boy grew
spotted, spoke, made
himself the enemy
of everything underfoot.

Hot Brown Babies

All the babies went brown to black
and back and forth with color
until it settled back according
to the laws of pigment
and sun
and difference.

And all their bones were made
to break under the unbearable,
and they were given souls
of soup
for they were toothless.

It was all a gift
or it was not,

for there was sameness
meant to bless, but
it did not.

Distinctions were made
by tint or hint of difference
and tribes no taller
than a crawl

armed themselves with twigs
and branch, and poked

out the eyes of newts and frogs

—and so began The Troubles.

Red Ochre

In future Portugal,
pale as a Lapp,

a nameless girl
made quiet conversation
with her fingers, red,

on the face of the boy black
as a Masai.

Red with burnt ochre,
each painted the other
until they were blood
red—the slip,
glistening—

hiding the Neandertal,
the Cro-Magnon until
these distinctions
were obscure and

adorned. *And he
commented on
her occipital
bulge,*

*and, she, flustered,
red-faced,*

she . . .

Yellow Woman

Technically,
  in the spectrum of light
  and by ordinary laws
  of nature,

  she should have been
  the color between green
  and orange, and complimentary
  to blue—a ripe lemon, an egg yolk

  —something controlled and routine,
  but she had more an olive sheen
  —and bold humor, and though
  the sea of her imagination was but
  the Bay of Biscay, Yellow
  Woman and her MtDNA
  didn't care. They were there
  for a swim.

  Not an odyssey, a whim.

  She'd spied the gulls
  and followed with her kit
  and stick.

  Done with living on offal
  quarried from the ice rubble
  at the great moraine
  of the Pyrenees,

  she swam.

Admix

LAW: Pigment is to place as tone
     or tint is to distance traveled
     epoch to epoch no matter
     the time taken, minding
     the weather.
     p.s. Movement is often mistaken for progress, and stasis
     for stagnation.

Migration tended toward north,
distinguished by, and characteristic of
its parallel (colorations of whiteness)
—a slow fade of skin to bone,
to two-tone, off whites,
later grays and eastern

unknowns; the common
blackish blue
keepsake kin kept
at a distance.

Virtue

LAW: The presence or absence of goodness
      —of which absence of a sense
      of self—the inability to
      distinguish a self
      in a context of
      other selves . . .

Has evil dress
as a small
lapse—

a sated
salamander
eating a spider,

a careless raven
feeding dropwort
to its bairn.

A boy
crushing
a toad.

Antipathy

What it was
was a shift in the moon's
slender light, its
shadow on the fen
knifing his face
to sinister,
to threat, to
threatening.

Then brother saw
brother in a new light.

Darker

Shadow in the flower heads
and teazle, up the leafy stems
and thistle to the waste land
and hedgerow, hooking
through the brush and broom,
combing into the deep
cup of fern and forest
harsh . . .

This will permit its decay
—the sedge, the brown bog,
        —the end of . . .

Nettle

In her single-minded way
she wondered:
was it her hybrid disposition
that had her fighting
over food and shade spot,
or was it just
the ordinary
discomfiture of being
upright and awkward,
thick-legged and
prone to bruised
bone, burns gotten
playing
with fire?

Was that it—that
and looking the fool?

Was all this
what had her cutting
her own forearm
with the chipped
obsidian tool,

wounding the enemy
within?

First Blood

Then, when teeth
were knives,

incisors tore
to neck bones
and blood
        —a bath—
was ordinary
as gore was decoration

—a rinse
of victory
—its reeky fragrance
seasoned the air.

Not sweet, not
overwhelming, nor

gory as we know it now
from movies,

but wondrous,

glistening
on all who came,
—on all their mouths
and tools.

Shame was not there, nor pride,
its stenchy bloom not there
to glisten
on all who came.

It was not there amongst them,
nor were they bathed with names
and causes yet
or blessed
with certainty.

Speech

Whether it was a weak larynx
or some predisposition to solitude, or a three
degree variation in a waval amplitude
in the range of a newly found voice
which caused it to sound
froggish

or whether it was by choice,
his language stuck in his throat

until this speechless Neandertal
ended his silence
and made, almost,
                    a word

Heard amongst the Cro-
Magnon interlopers as

            a threat.

Since, in the privacy of the Black
Forest, and, perhaps, somewhere
in France,

they'd been practicing
a word or two of their own

—so they killed the last of the species,
cheeky bastard that he was.

Fen

Everything was wet as a fish.

And the pointed sticks, one tipped
with chipped stone, the other bone,
slipped in their wet hands as
they poked the neutral air
between themselves,

and one boy cut the other,

the other boy cut the first

until they were stabbing,

making the small wounds that weaken.

And because their playfulness, their
laughter, did not know yet
to bleed out to
adrenalin,

they grinned as they fought, yet
the pointed sticks were driven such
that each could have found a frog's
belly even in the mist and fog.

So the beginning of their long death
came and they were both gone

suddenly; bog men
they were, and gone.

And we wonder still over their leeched bodies
and all their earth's irresolvable mysteries.

Berries

Yellow-headed or red,
bunched like berries sweet
and bitter, those boys
huddled on the strand
were not all blood
and disposition, their
wildness spilling out just
to be quarrelsome,
act deadly.

These fair times,
the moon quartered
on the morning's
horizon, the tide
out, the sea a toss
of ribbon, the boys
dig clams from
black mud beds,

they play
—forgetting fool's play
once honed to a taunt, forgetting
any killing memory

which has a hard-skinned boy
sticking a frog—

The
death of
someone
small
and

grand.

Grass

Those warriors,
their wars shelved,

their skills dormant
after death's near miss,

their wounds closed
without a mend,

would burn the wet
gray grass, pull its roots,
beat the ground with
sharp sticks,

drum over the mortal
thump of a fear-filled
heart's beat outside
its fallow room.

It was enough
to make farmers of them,
their pounding hearts
pulsing in their heads,
thrumming the neck's
strings, such
music, such

humdrum
—they wouldn't hear
any call to arms, or think
a cutting word, barely

could they cut the bloom
off earth's fresh face,

digging shallow graves
in narrow rows, planting
seeds like
bodies.

Chickpeas

Cicer arietinum. Not named for the wart
on Cicero's nose. The wart was named
for the chickpea.

They did without the winged or waxed
bean, ate their bitter vetch and barley, einkorn
wheat and emmer, all then nameless grains tasting
grassy
—the fancier vegetables not yet imagined—
they did not think the spear
of the asparagus exotic, the blood
seed of the tomato saucy, the garbanzo
erotic. Fussy, they were not, yet

they were tired of ruffage and easy
fruit harvested without a labor
worthy of its juice.

And not having discovered yet the tuber,
nor made a history
as the Irish would
with the potato,

theirs were futures imagined
without bull-headed famine, or
the narrow perimeter of
oppression.

They were the first in hope,

and farmed.

Gods

Much in those first few
hundred thousand years was slowly new.

At last, a first tool—more a point
than not, without even a first dimension
—only its curious impression,
    the indent.

When,

thousands of years blowing by,
a line is nicked into a schisty rock,
flakes fly one behind another,
bend into a second dimension
that first time as the nick
takes the curve . . .

Thousands of years
blowing by before circumference
—the concept

—and she's cupping her hands thinking:
in a thousand years: a bowl, and, he,

entwining his fingers, thinking
maybe in another thousand
—maybe longer—*a basket* . . .

Either, both, encompassing
the void.

Gods then, they.

ICE

Bridge

Back and forth in fathoms of air
across the land bridge
above which vapors and birds
swam where hence 10,000
plus-years fish would fly
and the sky would be wet
with the North Sea—

the exposed UK continental
shelf is tundra—sedge and berry
wintering at the edge
of frost and thaw.
Atlantis then,
might have been
some sleepy Cherbourg,

those Mesolithic French
Welsh-ish, those Rhinelanders
on the Thames more fish than fowl
(or not) give or take a meter
up or down, depending on
the atmosphere, and whether
or not the ice sheet was more
land than sea ice—whether
or not this ice was retreating

or it was us and them
backing away from the edge
of the last ice age unwilling,
any longer, to exploit the sea
mammals

—*whomever* they might have been,
back then,

when we crossed
the sea bed living a lie
in wait.

Doggerland

When the ice came and took the sea
it meant everything to me—

the ancestors not missing the abyss
of our futures; the ice giving them low
wet bottom land—that they had us
in their collective memory
—sweet genome guarding
the treasure that is us...

* * *

The North Sea waned,
left this verdant peninsula within
walking distance of France and Iberia,
—the Thames and the Rhine with their
common mouth, with lowlands
being uplands, distinctions between
over and under, sky
and sea obscured
by doubt.

Then, before hazards to shipping
and summer, we were bent to shape.

* * *

It would not even out, the weight
of the ice—the land tilting,
the ice scouring the soul's terrain.
Even-handedness, frostbitten,
lost its fingers; the bottom lands
where the bulk of us were stored
for the cold months, kept the Y
and kept the mitochondrial, kept
duality with its common mouth.

Vicinity

Names would not yet attach.

Selves were shells not put to the ear,
unheard—a sea of firsts, bewildering,
weather-borne.

And place, as well, came and went
without a foothold.

And, we, missing
  the small geographies
    of north or south,
      traversed
        diagonally.

In stepping
forth,

if a foot
was favored,
a shoulder swooned
to the spoilt foot, tipped the head
to the edge of its reach, the chin
a perch—or a poor means
of reckoning—sometimes
seen as an aggressive posture.

Burdened thus, twisted, we
moved away,
listed according
to the favored foot,

bent
toward a
hallowed
self.

***

Atlantic R1b—our genomic variant,
wandered south leaving
the Baltic-Russians, and
the North Sea-Baltics, amongst others.

The ice came and went.
The sea came home to Doggerland.

There is still a small memory
of Asian Kazakhstan, in the region
of our heart cut by the Volga River
that is our ancient homeland
in our most ancient heart.

Before the migration, before a thought of being
aboriginal or individual, before indigenous
was us

in the wide spare Russe,
the grassy cut-out plain which
the river made, has the alluvial

us, shallow-rooted.

Blind Meander

. . . and I saw three unclean spirits like frogs come out of the
mouth of the dragon and out of the mouth of the beast and out
of the mouth of the false prophet . . .

– Revelation 16

The law then, in rude society,
is heard wrongly,
has them follow the water or the wild
dogs, who follow the water
frogs until they've eaten them all.

This blind meander, its mouth
gaped, takes in the quenching lie
which has us believing before
belief begins—before
prophets implore us to follow.

No gods yet, either, in whose name
one might falsely prophesy.
Nor had we spirits of any sort,

though we'd begun to imagine
dragons—over our shoulder, of course,
—where we'd come from
because, we forgot quickly
where we'd come from
—what that meant
to who we were,

and so—with distance
came an abiding fright.

And while we still had our thin tolerance
to frost and thaw because our body mass
and our metabolic rate were such
—combined with the wrap of
the skinned beast's skin,

we now wished ourselves safe,
wished ourselves to sleep, wished
on our teeth—imagined fairy
and demon.

Unsettled

Imagining ourselves
done with migration, we
imagined ourselves
done, not loosed.

We did not flow or go easy.
We made such enemies
in our heads it pleased us
to name them

and give their antitheses
the names of gods.

Separate

Without the wobble
of rapid change—the quickstep
a fix for the misstep—the hazelnut
trees grew into thick cover,
the lime and the oak grew
old. *We* took hold.

What was it grew then
made us separate,
so specific we'd
differentiate, take *Three D*
as how we'd see.

How'd it come to be

—all this flex and reflex
uncommon to the red roe
deer, the pine martin,

common amongst us
living parallel to ourselves

always an island away
from a homeland
under a sea?

Myth / history

Must I stop lying, then, when the truth's
beneath a mound, flits through a henge?

Doesn't it bear telling, the story
having worked with the egg
about the womb, attaching
a fable to a history?

* * *

There was never a King and Queen who lived happily together,
but *that* never stopped the stories. Never a frog prince
with a lover who wasn't a frog. Or a toad blessed
with stories. Nothing stops a truth wending
its way to the lie . . .

Underworld

You would've hoped
the underworld was hard under,
stone rhyming with bone there,
as it did elsewhere—
but not sorrow with marrow.

A butcher's helper
would be thinking tallow
and light and warmth not sorrow
as he dressed a kill, a cow—no demon
but him about, skinning a new coat, no fear

wetting his nose hair, him rhyming bone
with stone, his finger bones, wrists
twisting other knuckles
against their joints.

All giving, forgiving, all rended none too soon
— all asunder red wet and reek

—that self amidst its beginning and ours.

Magic

I'm found somewhere in all their ancestral poems.

The one that begins: *He sleeps, we mustn't*
would have been difficult to imagine
given their nomadic lives, souls
migrating alongside cattle,
one minute disembodied,
the next attached, small
tether to a small hand
enough to bind.

Magic had a part in their lives.

Or some Basque witch
whom we'd offended
would've stopped
them dead

before they got to us.

Wort & Wen

Whether it was French or called Mediterranean
heath—or heather, for that matter, or gorse-
covered—the worst of the ground cover, or
whether or not the small pink or purple
flowers made it more moor
didn't matter

to the heathland butterfly or moth or
medicine woman bent to her pharmacy
pinching at the wortcunning, biting off
the nettle-tip.

This one *For the Loss of Cattle*, this
For the Water-Elf Disease, this
Against a Wen.

Busy she is against the moth,
and singing her charms for the practice

into the mouths and ears and wounds.

TOWNLANDS

Bouris

a townland

As we would tell it—
the first fish out of water
is a mackerel
out of Clew Bay
intent on legs
and a language.

He insinuates himself into a gene pool;
his Gaelic is shoddy, westernized,
a bit of the bog in its throaty
call to arms. Sticks, blackthorn, thick
as a neck, bring him upright, smelling
of the sea still, but passable, salt
splitting his lips, black Irish
heart unfibrillating, knees
like roundstones make their way
to Galway and some cocksure lie
will lay the groundwork for who we are.

Dallyriffle—

the first given name in Hibernia,

as in: "... stop dallyriffling ..." is dependent

on riffle for *a patch of waves or ripples,*
and dally: *act or move slowly*—was given casually to boys
and girls alike, who splashed blithely across the Irish Sea
during the Great Crossing when the sea was walkable.

A Gaulic or Celt translation would be slash
marks on a tree, cuts in stone. Unspeakable.

A guttural rendition coughed out as O Cingeadh,
anglicized as O'Kinga, became King.

—We are not those water-dobbing kings.

Drift

It had rifted—the Iberian
Peninsula, twining anti-
clockwise in post-Eocene,
disturbing the horizon,
building a Bay of Biscay
by early Miocene.

A way for Viking ships
to reach the Loire, the Garronne,
—into the gut of France, except
the swoddies, those warm
water eddies which schemed,
took a boat
to Aquitaine,

where this wobble-legged
boy, half Manx, half myth
settled in   out
of the Isle of Man
and some distant old
and violent history

which he didn't know,

adrift as he was, with
the small wish to fish
—or farm

some fertile French daughter
of Yellow Woman.

Natterjacks

There would have been one or two snakes
—adder or Irish king drowned in the ankle deep Irish Sea
when we came over—

 If no snakes, a memory of snakes.

No frogs, except one, and common.
One toad—the natterjack, without teeth.
One smooth newt, skittish.
One lizard, British.

Newbies

From round stone to round stone
they wobbled, bits of bog between
their toes unnoticed, farmers not yet
farmers nor bound yet
to a Clachan

or to dry stone boundary
walls double stacked
for stability, long life.

Not bound, even, to single stones
stacked one on one and loose,
such that skittish sheep stayed put.

And though the limits of townland
and tenancy had not yet been imposed,
these would one day surround
the arable and graze land, would
cause grief immeasurable, settle
some things, leave
others unsettling.

No *fuchsia* yet, either,

    or trumpeting
montbretia easing tired men
into commonage.

Ebb / Flow

It wasn't easy, ebb / flow, no come or go
the same as when you'd left. It was more wobbly.

We'd all stay till Queenstown.

Our feet would dry and flatten, we'd settle in
until the instep bucked, the spongy bottoms
of our feet arched—and we had our wherewithal,
wouldn't stay put.
                        We left again for no good reason.

From the north, we riffled down,
followed the Shannon's cut, or the East's sea coast,

avoided the West. These were MacCartaith, O Beollain,
                        the new Murphys.

And, as if condemned to Van Diemen's Land,
the Mag Fhionnin, O Clochartaigh, O hEidehin's,
even the Greenes before they were Greenes
went West long before Cromwell gifted it,
winching themselves around the Twelve Pins or
slipping through Joyce Country to Connemara.

Some, even, by sea, around Slyne Head
to Dog's Bay, by land then, to Errisbeg West.

All this while O hAonghusa made
themselves Hennesseys in Munster,
waited for the push of Anglo-Normans
to displace them.

All this after the Conneelys—our weak historians,
whittled their ancient histories on sticks, buried them in bogs
        with their bog men.

All this while O Fearghusa taught himself quackery,

imagined himself physician to the high and mighty
O Maille.

Henge

The architects
did not
use the shell middens
in Portugal as go-by's.

Our stone megaliths were our own.

Nothing Portuguese ours
but the tint of fishers' blood
—the stone flags ours
entirely,
their rich paint leached
out of the great grave

—not the new swaley graves in bogs
with their little wisp of dead
and shallow history.

Our dead reach through
—build in our head.

Wild Sedge

Common names were uncommon: no
lady fern ragged robin sally willow
—low to middle to high, maneuvered
through, cut without contemplation;
some for thatch, some for kindle
or war stick.

And while it was commonly
known that wild sedge
was handy for pillowing
a tired head, it was uncommon
that wild sedge warblers
nesting in cups of grass mistook
the gaped mouth of a napper
for home
      —yet the phrase:

      . . . *Bird-mouth* (also *crow's foot*)
      that interior angled notch cut
      into a timber ' . . . *for the reception*
      of the edge of another timber . . . '

The beginnings, then, of joinery
and carpenters, "the beginnings
of the hurried end of the Forests
Dense

      . . .*so dense that if*
      a man mounted a tree branch
      at Fairy Hill on the seashore
      at Bunowen, he could travel
      from branch to branch without
      touching the ground until he
      reached Glan Bawn . . . "

Pagan

Our priests were gone, gods shrunk.
Our wells had dried, the trees dead.
No more holy water out of holy wells.
No holy trees, nor wicked teas
a druid brewed.

The new priests good for nothing
but tea water. Their God grew
like a fish story.

We, fishers, with our haddock faces
and herring legs, who'd tweezed
between the eggs of the cod,
to find the pearly best of God
—forgot
the molecular past, forgot
the open arms of the hawthorn,
forgot men living on the acorn

—or was it nuts and apples, was it a yew
or an oak meant to be a firm strong god . . .

Water Babies

All the children born by then were dipped
in water. All the children born before
dipped in water. The druids leached
their water out of stone;

the new priests, at first, tried spit,
which left generations born
with phlegmy dispositions
sitting at the feet of authority.

Some grandmothers used fish oil
or fished the dry holy wells,
and put the grit in the corners
of each eye, meant
to seal up infant tears.

Some sucked a breath
out of the baby's mouth
to ward off fate
—or was it to keep them clear of Dublin?

The Wren

The wrens came and perched on the Irish drums,
and their tapping and noise aroused the English
soldiers, who fell on the Irish troops and killed
them all . . .

                                    –Lady Wilde

Before that there was their anti-Papist rhetoric—
their noisy churr churr betraying Saint Stephen.

And long before Cromwell,
when Ice Age ice was slush,
there were wren boys
killing winter wrens
—the Druids' bird—

Old World hens
sacrificed to a lost memory
before there was that memory.

The Kings of Desmond

There's no blood of the Kings of Desmond that's ours.
Nor are we the Sourbreath McCarthy bunch.
We're the big-boned, knob-nosed distant ones
with cab driver faces who minded our business
in Tipperary and elsewhere,
as if we'd be left alone to outlast
the faction fights and the Normans.

Blind wrong we were, and pushed into Cork with the rest,
who still look askance at us. You'll see them do it in Southie
—on East Broadway—that over-the-shoulder look they give

as if to say—*what's this . . . the Lower End coming up!*

when they ought wonder, *is this one of Black Hugh's hard boys*
with an eye out for Burkes or Ormondes,

anything belatedly Irish.

Royals

It wasn't invaders split us into rotty fiefdoms,
rootless kings outnumbering the whitefly.
It wasn't Saxon or Norseman or the shite
Norman ate the liver out of a Kingdom.

It wasn't wives or bitter princes lost the Crown,
or Burke kept us out of Burke's *Peerage*,

had the Berry woman, Kathleen—the stair scrubber, in steerage.

It was Connemara boys with pointed sticks, one tipped
with chipped stone, the other bone,
gripped in their wet hands,

one boy cutting the other, the other boy cutting the first . . .

Pattern Day

Is Saints Peter and Paul's Day
at the fair of Ballynahinch
—or was it at Roundstone,

or was it the Pattern of Maum Ean
(Maum Ean—the gorge of the birds)
held on Garland Sunday,

where Greeora Mannion had his nose bitten off
by one of the tribesman of one of the wildest
tribes in creation?

. . . These were the two greatest fights of modern times . . .
between the Joyces of Joyce Country and the Malleys of Maam . . .

> *The other fight began between the Kings of*
> *Errisbeg and the Mannions of Cashel. The Kings*
> *were great, stout men, but the Mannions were*
> *the tallest men, I dare say, in Connacht.*
> *This was surely the battle of gods*
> *and giants, and they fought on until*
> *the shades of night separated them,*
> *nor was the fight decided on that day,*
> *for it was to be renewed at the next*
> *fair at Ballynahinch.*

And wives followed
the wounded, thinning
the number with stone
-filled stockings.

This, how we distinguished ourselves.

Gifting

It was not the knack for mending wounds
made O'Malleys' physicians out of the shaky O'Fearghuis,
nor was it the Old Head Gordon woman has us
fertile as a barley field after turnips. It wasn't
McCarthy devouring the bitter
Lonergans, either, gave us
a taste for the sour.

Before there was an errant father to blame
for who we are or what we've done
—or not done

Before there was a father to blame for his son,

there is our primeval Mother Black unsettling
herself in East Africa

for momentum's sake.

Uncles

Augustinians, schooled
in Salamanca, smuggled
to the strand at Inisfail,
their father's lugger
under half-sail, two
great prow lug sails
finding the wind.

At half-sheet,
she'd not
be caught, not with
our three black-haired boys,

their druid ribs mooring
their pagan hearts, their
perjured souls.

Aunty

As cousins go,
the pirate, Grace O'Malley,
was distant.

But since the leech O'Fergus
left the wound of her mouth
open,

it's likely she whispered that she favored us.

Worry Bother Mither

She had always the wobble
of the earth to contend with
—the shimmer felt in the swale
between the ridges of her brain
where the mitochondrial rift was

—that chasmic separation
with its layered geology shifting
when the sun or the moon tugged.

Not a tide, with its pleasing constant
of come and go   come and go
—never lifting up, always bound
downwards toward worry,

as mothers worry, birth to death.

Packman

Pat Malley—Paddy Paurick Arida or
Hugh O'Malley, Patrick Aoidh O'Malley
of Shraugh, last packman of West Mayo.

One and the same and all liars he was

—and all the more so after he became a cattle jobber.

> *He lost much blood in faction fights,*
> *lived to be one hundred and twelve,*
> *died in a state of innocence and*
> *2nd childhood,*

Was forgiven for working tooth and nail
for the Brownes of Westport.

Descended from Malachie of the Broad Sword
who slew many of the Brownes of Westport,

and so, we might imagine, Mr. Browne
imagining the packman's allegiance
as more than it was,

but it wasn't.

DEATH AT DOO LOUGH

Dark Lake (1849)

For the Daltons and McHales of Wastelands,
the Dillons, the Flynns, the Gradys and the rest . . .

It is a bitter Friday, the 30th of March. Another
Starving Day—the sun, eaten by the mist
hooding Mweelrea's mountain, has the day
looking as if it's to be hung by the British
hangman.

The peasants are uprooted by the hope of a workhouse ticket
or an allotment of three pounds corn.

The Indian corn, America's, rough as nettle husk
stales in warehouses. The workhouse chits
are bundled in drawers.

These poor—are those who must qualify as paupers,
and move as might a scourge of insects toward light
of morning, toward the guardians
of the Poor Law Union,
of which, two,

a Colonel Hogrove, and a Mr. Lecky
will decide their fates
over lunch.

As a blight, the Death of Sheep and Cattle Plague
compares and, these Irish poor in droves,
a blight themselves, bend their mass
toward Louisburg and relief

at the hand of the Relief Officer,
who does not have his books ready
—sends them to Delphi Lodge,
twelve miles through the wilds
to pass inspection.

* * *

That night, wet and threadbare,
they settle at the fronts of houses
—these skeletal things—
their remains unwinding like shadow
atmospheres down
to stoop and niche as might
the town stray hound haul down
herself at night.

The next morning, among the dead, the living
rise and walk, four hundred of the starving
peasantry lift themselves, lean to Delphi
Lodge and judgment.

> . . . *They wade through the swollen Glankeen,*
> *climb to the brow of the precipice overhanging*
> *Captain Houston's house, descend to a river far*
> *deeper than the Glankeen, are cold, and wet and*

> . . . *the vice-guardians, Hogrove and Lecky*
> *will not have their lunch disturbed. And the people*
> *sit down in their damp and miserable rags amongst*
> *the pine trees and expire.*

> *And when the two gentlemen condescend to see the peasantry,*
> *they refuse to grant them relief or tickets to the workhouse,*
> *so the fearful journey has all been in vain.*

> *Night approaches. They set out once more for the place of their birth.*

Again they ascend to the valley between the hills
and the Mweelrea Mountains cut
by the two rivers—
its black lake fills
the mountain pass, unpassable
except by goat path—now mud
and shearing
off in the wind and rain
—a hailstorm blinding
them . . .

the wind veers round to the north-west,
their cold rags stiffen like cold sheet iron.

In their weakness they begin to fall.

When they reach the terrible spot called the Stroppabue
on the brow of the cliff, tremendous squalls sweep them
by the score into the lake. Those who try to climb the steep
slanting stroppa lose their hold, fall as they climb.

The corpses fall into the dark lake.

And tomorrow, gangs of starving men will come to the corpse-strewn
trail to gather

and carry neighbors to the glen cut by the last ice
of the last ice age, enough soil there to scour
out a shallow grave. And spare room
for requiem.

The few survivors perish on the southern bank of the river.
On the next morning, the trail from Glankeen to Houston's house
is covered with corpses as numerous as the sheaves of corn in
an autumn field . . .

. . . and there is no earth along the goat track deep enough for graves
save in the little glen . . . so they bury them in pits

just as on a battle field.

Now, set nearby, is an imperfect celtic cross, its edges
gnarled as if some hungry thing has gnawed at stone.

KATHLEEN

Kathleen (1899)

Put yourself in her place:

She is ten years old

—a pink-bodied daughter of primeval
Yellow Woman pretending to be Irish

—ten thousand years removed from a hint
of who our mother is.

In the ruin of a hedge school,
she inks a history on her arm.

Under the yew tree at St Mary's,
she pinches blackberries, rubs juice
on her cheeks, repeats a past under
her breath, rubs her palm clean
before it's seen:

> *This will be why they'll paint their bodies*, she says.

* * *

This morning, while her brother James imagines
he's driving a spike for the Boston & Maine,

Kathleen sees herself in East Africa . . . far from her cottage garden,
on Mynish Island, Galway, where an Ard Bay breeze,
coming south, riffles her savannah grasses;

she overturns dozens of ground beetles,
waits for the African sun to cook them . . .

* * *

Sunday. She will be picking wild flowers
and stones. She says the flowers are wild, but
they're not. Nor are the stones, though

they're not tame. The flowers, *bloody
cranesbill, foxglove* are too pink
and warm for wild, the *dog rose*
and *dog violet* too faithful
to the garden.

The stones have their veil of white
montbretia, which she won't bother,
and not bother the *wall pennywort*
in the pockets of the stone walls
which bound her, though she will
pick up the bottom stones,

unsettle some, the wall.

Marsh thistle's safe from her
as is the *bride of the druids.*

* * *

This nightshade didn't offer shade at night,
didn't often offer blight, except the once,
leafless, spotted as toads they came.

Her Mum won't have the potato grow
in the field. She'd sooner
grow stones.

Smuggler (1900)

Not even grandchildren knowing
you were hated have room for you.

Now they'll know, Joseph, how
I smuggled you into my heart.

This, long before you'd see me dance;
before the priest worked to keep us apart.

Before my father imagined twenty
cows and a bull as dowry.

In the cemetery where we played,

was I tying strips of red
to the hawthorn tree,

you ready with your dull blade,

the tree with its snowy cloud
of tiny flowers? Was it May,
then, when first we were
at odds?

You, fast to make the unlucky cut,
me, swearing you off,
as I would often do.

You could not wait for May eve,
then pluck a branch or two
for us.

You took it down as wattle wood and fodder,
as you'd been taught, bunched
the flowering sprigs
for me.

Albert, Duke of Saxe-Coburg and Gotha (1901)

Their Queen is dead. She was a good mum.

But not to us. My father thought to write
the Duke of Edinburgh and express regrets
until Mum reminded him the Duke, as well,
was dead.

Who was the Duke to you, I said
—and brother Edward winked, hurried out.

Mum, between father and the door,
having been here often, determined
to give a good show.

He was prince till demoted.
Spent his life taking a step back . . .

Bridget, stop your foolishness . . !

. . . all the way to Germany . . .
. . . a German Duke at the end . . .

He was a humble nice fellow, Bridget,
a fine sailor . . . and did his best.

Ah, Kathleen, listen to your father, now.
He'll say 'twas he and little Affie saved the West . . .

We'd done this before, mother stage directing
while I listened as if it were fresh news—

> *. . . I suffer Ireland was scarcely ever in a worse state*
> *of poverty,* he began, *than it was in the spring, & the*
> *summer is far worse. We formed a relief committee in*
> *Carna . . . all the clearing out of the steamers calling to*
> *Kilkerien Bay fell to my lot. We had as many as eight*
> *steamers and the Duke of Edinburgh's steamer yacht . . .*
> *I have frequently talked to the Duke, and he is a humble,*
> *nice fellow. . . .*

Joseph (1902)

It is all Joseph and the body
of water that he is.

The Archbishop is dead.
Victoria in the Royal
Mausoleum.

Authority's
dying off.

We'll soon forget
Bridget Greene &
James Berry.

My brothers may stay.
My sisters will emigrate,
—not Lena
—she'll stay. And Michael,
the post man, too.

I'll go.

So, Joseph,   Joseph, come to me,
                we have work . . .

You are my body of water
my body of Christ.

Novella (1903)

The ideas in my head, the ones
my father imagines happen there
because I read novels,

happen there in my novella

as I live it. It's a dreary year
so far. Nothing at all new here,

so I'm writing this from Kazakhstan,
where it is much more drear
but there are lots of cousins

and black tea,
and no hope of change.

No one leaves as they wish,
the borders inch in
toward a dark center
which is malignant;
something Russian.

This is a harsh place
and familiar;
one I think I should never want
to forget, but I must.

I ought not to have an ancient
homeland competing with
the one I will soon leave.

It confuses whatever history I
might make

orphaned from a past.

Egyptian (1904)

I would think we were all Egyptian once.

Attending the Punchestown Races
whenever we pleased, worshiping
dogs and cats, swimming,
at our leisure, in the River
of Life.

I would think the King and Queen
have a life much like that,
visiting at Lisemore
as they please,

not a thought to emigrating.

1905

Since 1851, almost 4 million people have left the island.

On a good day, when the tide is out, I can walk
from Mynish to the rise and fall of the insignificant
islets and strait that take me to the strand on the pip
of shore passing for the mainland
—the rip rap roundstoned beach washed up
at the foot of Carna
when some little Ice Age came and went.

I'm leaving
with or without Joseph.

When my sisters send enough for passage,
I'll go to Cork and Queenstown, breaking Bridget's
heart.

All that to say that this is a wild and mountainous district,
famines common as failure. The bay of Ardwest
has lead wind in, seldom out, as if to say,
we'd never leave but to fish.

I've spun no yarn, made not a stocking.
It is a bad fit, me and Moyrus, a parish in
the barony of Ballinahinch, county of Galway,
the province of Connaught.

In Ard bay are the ruins of Ard castle,
of which I would once have been mistress
and queen, ruler of heath and hedge,
lizard and toad, faeries and fallen angels.

*Now, I will be the Berry woman, late of Boston
and its labours.*

Queenstown (1908)

It is the first of May, and I am off to Clifden

and the railroad,

and the world's end

according to Bridget, who fears
she'll never see her daughters again.
  We'd send her passage
  if she'd come.

I'm sailing alone on a White Star steamer.
Brother James has gone ahead, arrived, is
amongst the New Jersey cousins.

In Queenstown, St. Coleman's steeple
is missing. I notice, too, all Ireland
disappearing
out the railroad's window.

I notice, now, the hem of my short past
unraveling, each foot forward snaring
the threads such I seem to be
     wobbling.

Steady, now, the ancestors whisper.

I wish a sister or two were near.

This is dear work, moving
the mitochondrial across
the sea.

* * *

This fog this morning disappears

all Ireland.

The harbor disappears.

There is a lead wind out.

The sea scissors over the land.

St. Coleman's steeple appears.

I'm barely out of view and
Bishop Browne's at requiem for the lost
at sea.

There's a fog
this morning

as my Ireland

disappears.

In Basque Spain, where I'm once from
after squeezing through the little isthmus

of the great migration, near dying
before the chickpea and the pointy
chert were in my kit, I bit

my tongue to keep from saying aloud
how fright was

not enough to keep me

still . . .

NOTES

Wild Sedge. The definition of Bird's-mouth is from Webster's Revised Unabridged Dictionary of the English Language 1919 edition. The second quotation is from The Adventures of Foranan O'Fergus in Tales of the West of Ireland by James Berry.

Pattern Day. The quotation is from Berry's The Rescue of Nula O'Flaherty.

Dark Lake is essentially a borrow from Berry's Death at Doo Lough and liberally quoted.

Albert, Duke of Saxe-Coburg and Gotha. The end quotation is from Berry's letter to his daughter, Mary, date June 1, 1880.

Dicko King was born at Carney Hospital in South Boston, and raised in St. Margaret's parish in Dorchester during the last of the grand and mythical eras presided over by tribes of feral children—when adventures could be had beyond the watchful eyes of a mother or father, and despite strictures and wounds inflicted by priest or nun.

Dicko is the son of Mary Alice McCarthy whose people are from Cork and Tipperary. His father is Richard King out of County Mayo and Galway and descended from the legendary physician, Foranan O'Fergus, who slew the Fiend of the Lake. Before returning to Southie at the age of twelve, Dicko relinquished sovereignty over a small band of wild boys whose townland was Edison Green with its imposing and venerated druidic god of an elm tree—the 'Greenie Tree.' Near the barren elm he presided, for the last time, over the winter ritual of the yule tree bonfire—a pyramid of flame and pungent smoke rising above the sacred ground of the Green into the Twelfth Night's sky.

Dicko's poems have appeared out of nowhere, some of them published in *Prime Number, Cactus Heart, Portland Review* and *Straylight.*

He is a finalist for The Louise Bogan Award.

He lives with his wife, Treva, in Phoenix.